CU00834623

SISTERS INCARNATED
Adapted from the filmscript TRILOGY
in two- acts by Alfred Vassallo

Katie /Louise Burrows	27 years Brunette/Blonde
Doctor Craig Flack	Middle-aged
David James	30 yr Louise's boyfriend
Anthony Harding	25 yr Louise's flirt
Inspector Alan Head	
Sergeant Green	

Act 1
The house of Katie and Louise Burrows. A Lounge.
Scene 1
Louise Burrows speaking to her boyfriend on the phone.
Scene 2 - One week
Katie Burrows meets David James.
Scene 3 -Two weeks later
Louise Burrows and Doctor Craig Flack
Scene 4 -
Louise and Kate Burrows in argument.
Act 2
The house of Katie and Lilly
Burrows. A Lounge.

ACT ONE - SCENE ONE

(We find Anthony sitting on an armchair and Louise is sitting on his lap. They are kissing passionately)

ANTHONY
(Pulls her away a bit)
We'll better stop. What if your sister comes back now?

LOUISE
She won't be back yet. I know Kate, when she goes shopping in town she stays till lunchtime.
(She grabs him again and kisses him but he resists)

ANTHONY
Stop it I said, is that why you called me to come here. You know I am not feeling comfortable in this house. If you wish we can go to my flat now!

LOUISE
You're a fucking coward.
(She moves away from him and lights a cigarette)
What's wrong in having some fun? May be you like men, is that it?

ANTHONY
No of course not. How can you say that after last night?

LOUISE
What about last night? For me it was a forgettable night. You don't know how to please a woman. Bang bang bang and it's all over.

ANTHONY
In that case why did you call me this morning?

LOUISE
Not to fuck you that is for sure. I wanted Katie to come in a find us together. She's so goody, goody and full of scruples I wanted to give a shock.

ANTHONY
You're a wicked bitch, you know that?

LOUISE
I know and I love it.
(She giggles)
Do you want a drink?

ANTHONY
(Stands)
I rather be going. I have many things to do.

LOUISE
Please yourself.
(She goes to a sideboard and pours herself a drink)
And please don't call me again, I don't want to see you any more.

ANTHONY
(As he moves out)
Don't worry, you're a freak!
(Exists)

(Louise with her the glass in one hand and a cigarette on the other she sits down and laughs)

LOUISE
Call yourself a man?
(She pauses, drinks and smokes. Takes out her mobile phone from her pocket and starts to tap some numbers)

Yes of course it's me. Did you expect someone else? Ah, that is better. Do you want me to send you my picture? Yes, in the nude. You would love that will you? Why? **(She laughs)**You can do better than that. Don't you get tired playing by yourself? Keep talking you turn me on!....Yes I tell you what I'm wishing.....Don't be impatient...

Here we go....Me and you laying side by side by the seaside watching the waves rolling by...all of a sudden you put your hand on my thighs and being to stoking them...Now my mind is completely changed and want you do do more......You start using your fingers and I'm loving it....What?   No, I think that's is enough for today....Maybe tomorrow we make love, it will be much better? **(Laughs)** You have to do it yourself because you're not going to see me today....Bye.

(She puts her mobile in her pocket)
(The land-line telephone starts to ring, lazily she picks up the receiver and listen)
Oh it's you Doctor, No she's not in yet, she's out shopping. Why? You see her more often these days? Why? Of course it is my business she's my sister....You don't like me don't you. Of course it does, it has to do with that. My father is at the end of his life....In hospital laying there, wasting, poor daddy. I know......When next week? Yes I tell her. You're coming here to see here? Why? Because I want to know? Oh I hate you doctor.
(Stands up, puts away her mobile back into her pocket and exists.

BLACKOUT

ACT ONE - SCENE TWO
One week later Katie is writing in her diary.

KATIE
It has been a week since father was cremated. Today I am alone in this huge house. Louise is out on a shopping spree, and trying to seduce men, even though she has got a steady boyfriend. Since his funeral I have looked at many family photos, especially those of Louise and father. They were always having fun while I sat beside mother who her only joy in life was knitting. Yet I knew what was going on between them. It's disgusting. Immoral and taboo. Poor mother she was so innocent, so weak. She never suspected the evil in Louise, my spoilt sister, I could kill her. Her sweet little face corrupted him, and he a fool that he was fell for her. She did not fool me though, I knew the darkness behind her face, I knew her unlimited evilness of her soul.

(There is the sound of the door bell and Katie with great calmness she closes her diary, puts it away in a her with the pen. And slowly exits towards the front door. After a while she walks in with David James, Louise's boyfriend.)

DAVID
Is Louise not ready?

KATIE
Sit down Mr. James, please
have a seat there.
(She points to the armchair.)

DAVID
(sits)
Can you call her for me please!

KATIE
She is not here.

DAVID
What do you mean, we were going to the Movies this evening.

KATIE
I told you she is not in the house. She left about an hour ago. Don't ask me where because I do not know.

DAVID
You don't know? She went out? But you're her sister?

KATIE
Yes, in fact we are twins not identical but we are.

DAVID
Yes, I noticed that. Honestly Miss, where did she go?

KATIE
(Ignores the question)
I know what you're thinking. You never thought that tin sister can look so differently from each other. I never had the temptation too dress like her, paint my face and talk seductively like her. You don't know anything Mr. James

DAVID
I don't know what you mean.

KATIE
Truly I do not know where she is, but I can guess.

DAVID
Guess?

KATIE
My sister is a weird girl. Unusual and unpredictable.

DAVID
But she seems so distress and upset by her father's
death.

KATIE
I doubt if you truly understand her? Do you. You don't
even know what she's like. That is why I opened the
door for you instead of living you pushing the button
until you got tired and left.

DAVID
(Confused and impatient)
What do you mean? Am I missing something here?

KATIE
You're missing a lot Mr. James, quite a lot.

DAVID
It is seems to me you don't like your sister.

KATIE
Like her? I loathe her. Yes I hate her.

DAVID
Is that why you telling me these things about her?

KATIE
No that is not the reason. My reason is kind and from
my heart.

DAVID
Say again please?

KATIE
**(She picks a photo from the table and hand it to
David)**
There look at that picture. She was sister then my
sister. But look carefully at her. At her gesture, her
pose, even then she was trying to attract his attention.

Can you notice how she is pressing so hard against him?

DAVID
(Stands and gives her back the photo and walks away. He pauses and turns facing Katie.)
I don't quite understand. What are you telling me?

KATIE
Are you really that stupid….Sorry, I didn't mean that. But surely you are not stupid, you can see what that photo suggests to you?

DAVID
No I don't see anything.

KATIE
Obviously love has blinded you.

DAVID
Yes I love her but what of it?

KATIE
Mr James my sister is evil.

DAVID
Evil?

KATIE
Yes, I think you should know that.

(David stands still lost for words)

Even as a child Louise was vicious, unkind and disobedient But above all she was cunning. Yet my stupid father, my daddy worshipped her and she took advantage of that. When she was sixteen she seduced him.

DAVID
(Becoming angry)
I don't know what you're trying to do and I do not want to hear any more.

KATIE
It was no long after that when mother died. They said she overdosed herself with sleeping pills, but I know for sure she killed her. It was Louise, she managed to put extra pills in her warm milk.

DAVID
(Agitated)
If what you're saying is true, how can you stay in the same house living with her?

KATIE
I haven't another place to go and live and after all this is half my house too. So now I keep to myself. I hardly talk to her or see her at all. In fact I try to avoid her as much as possible. Now I got used to it and ignore what's happening in this house.
(There is a long pause as they stare at each other)
You don't believe me, do you?

DAVID
(He walks towards her and stops very close)
Miss Burrows I do not know what to say!

KATIE
Mr.James Louise uses her evil charm to capture the souls of others. By her own admission she laughs and says that Satan guides her.

DAVID
You don't really expect me to believe this? Do you?

KATIE
But you must believe me. I am telling you the truth.
You see, Louise's soul is damned for good. And I
cannot help her. But I can help you before you're cage
by her evilness forever.

DAVID
(Sympathetically)
I'm afraid you are the one who needs help.

KATIE
(She burst out laughing and walks away)
How naive you are.
(Crying)
Do you really thing she cares for you. She lies to you.
She laughs at you.

DAVID
(Walks to the exit)
I'm sorry but I have to leave now.

KATIE
(As he is about to exit she burst out loudly)
I know all about you and her in that hotel. I know what
happened there.

DAVID
(Turns and face her)
She told you about that?

KATIE
(Ashamed and calmly)
Yes. She told me everything. Gloated and bragged
how she was able to corrupt you. Mr. James, my sister
enjoys inflicting pain. Somehow she persuaded you to
share her perversion. Are you still medicating your
back from those scratches you received? Do you
believe me now?
(David nods embarrassingly to Katie)

Then you are saved Mr. James. I have freed you from evil.
(David exits hurriedly. Katie sits down, takes out her diary and pen and writes)
I have met Mr. David James and freed him from Louise. One good deed for the day.

BLACKOUT
End of scene two

ACT ONE-SCENE THREE
Two weeks later - an afternoon

DOCTOR
I didn't expect to see you.

LOUISE
(Flirting)
I know you expected my sister. But instead you have got me. Isn't it not better, instead of that old frump?

DOCTOR
I am surprised at you. I really am. You have no sense of privacy. No sense of morals, nothing at all.

LOUISE
So?....
(Pause)
You want a drink?

DOCTOR
No thank you.

LOUISE
(Moves to the sofa in a sexual attitude and sits down seductively.)
Oh doctor, I know why you are here. This visit is about me isn't it. You came to see Kate because you were concerned about what she told you about me? I know what she told you about me I was listening on the extension line in the other room.

DOCTOR
Oh, I see.

LOUISE
Come and sit down.
(The doctor moves to sit on the armchair).
Oh no doctor, no there, her.

(She taps the sofa beside here, the doctor moves slowly and sits close to her)
That's better Doctor, much better. So once again it is just a wasted visit. Why do you come really? Don't tell me you're doing it with Kate?

DOCTOR
(Tries to stand by she stops him)
If you're going to talk nonsense….

LOUISE
Now, now Doctor,
(Strokes his hair)
You are being a naughty boy….But you wanted t see me, I know that and here I am Doctor Craig Flack….You want me instead, I am looking forward for a good fuck from you…..

DOCTOR
You know I cannot do these things, I get is that what you want to happen to me? Do you want to be chucked out of my profession.

LOUISE
Of course not, I only want your dick!

DOCTOR
That is enough and enough. Why are you doing this? You know you are not…..

LOUISE
I am what you want me to be and don't say another word.
(She zips his mouth)

DOCTOR
Did you destroy Kate's room?

LOUISE
Yes I did. Why shouldn't I? I know Kate won't talk
about me when I'm in the house.
(She strokes his forehead)
And here I am.

DOCTOR
Please....Please do not do this, otherwise....

LOUISE
Otherwise what, doctor? Why should she stick her
fucking nose in my affairs?

DOCTOR
But you are....

LOUISE
Shut up doctor, I am in control now, not you. You
came to see Kate but instead you are facing me,
Louise. The most sexy woman, the most voluptuous
one which can give you the most incredible fuck of
your life.
(There is a big pause the doctor just stares at her.)
But then again Kate have everything in order by now.

DOCTOR
I don't know what you're talking about.
(SILENCE)
Truly, I don't.
(Another pause)
This hatred has to stop. Eventually you will destroy
yourself.

LOUISE
I don't think so, Doc, I am what I am and nobody is
taken anything away from me, least of all the bitch
sister of mine Kate. Besides, doctor, it is all in Kate's
hand. She has this hatred towards me, and that is the

only way she can live with. If she stops hating me she dies of craving.

DOCTOR
Craving?

LOUISE
Yes craving, she yearns for the sperm to splash on her face, for the man who eats her vagina, that what Kate's want but she doesn't know how to go about it. And I do. She is jealous of me, doctor. Because I can fulfil my sexual desires when ever I please.
(Stops abruptly. She walks away and stops as though she is thinking of something new. She stand still. Then she turns around slowly and look at the doctor. She walks towards him and stops opposite him)
You know doctor, you are a handsome man and I don't mind if you suck me all over.
(The doctor stands and walks away)
Did that bother you doctor? Do I make you nervous and trying to hide your hard on?

DOCTOR
(Moves to the exit)
I don't think we can take this any further.

LOUISE
(Stands)
What's the matter doc? Are you still a virgin? Or is it that you don't like girls?

DOCTOR
(As he exists)
I will call upon Kate soon.

LOUISE
(Follows him to the door and shouts)
We don't need you any more Doctor.

(Pause)
Don't come here any more. We don't need you any
more, you are obsolete from our lives.
And fuck you too.!

BLACKOUT
End of scene three

ACT ONE - SCENE FOUR
One week later - morning

KATIE
It's good of you doctor to come again after the humiliation you've got from LOUISE.

DOCTOR
I am here to see you, Kate. I don't want to hear about your sister.

KATIE
But she's the reason for my predicament. I cannot do anything without her criticising and bullying me.

DOCTOR
I don't know what to say any more. I have explained to you many times. Forget about Louise, she doesn't exist.

KATIE
(Upset)
What do you mean she doesn't exist. Are you crazy? You spoke to her here last week.

DOCTOR
Yes I did.

KATIE
So?

DOCTOR
Nothing, I do not want you to get upset again. All I want to know if you are taking the medicine I gave you regularly? That is the important thing.

KATIE
Yes I do as prescribed.

DOCTOR
(Stands)
Good, I have to go now because I have other appointments.

(We hear the voice of Louise)
Is he still here? Kate

KATIE
Yes he is, and don't come downstairs please.

DOCTOR
(Ignoring all that)
As I said Kate don't miss those pills, without them your problem will escalate.

KATIE
Yes of course and thank you for coming.

(The Doctor Exists)
(Shouts at the direction to were the voice of Louise came)
He is gone now, and please don't come and disturb me I have a lot to do this morning.
(There is no answer).

(She takes out her diary from her pocket, sits and write)

KATIE
This morning we had a terrible row when LOUISE realised I invited the doctor to visit.She knows I tell him everything. She came at me like a ferocious tigress and I locked myself in the room. She kept banging and kicking on the door for ages calling me all sorts of things. After a while she went back to her room and fell

into a drunken sleep. I am fed up with this and something has to be done about it. I don't understand how this can be happing to me. I am on prescribed drugs because of her, because I cannot stand the sight of her. I have to get rid of her, and soon.

BLACKOUT

END OF ACT ONE

ACT TWO
The lounge of the Burrows. A day later

KATIE
(Writing on her diary)
Yesterday I had a good day. A very good day. I was alone all day while Louise left the house early and didn't return until night time. Only God knows what she was up to. I don't care. Being alone in this house it's like heaven. I had a chance to look over the family photos and rekindle those wonderful memories I had with daddy and with mummy in the kitchen.
Then I prepared lunch for me and read my favourite books all day. I don't know what time did Louise return.

(The door bell rings. She stands and puts her diary in her pocket and exits to the front door. We can hear some indistinct chatter and then Katie returns with Inspector Alan Head and Sergeant Green)

KATIE
Please sit down. Can I offer you tea or coffee.
(They both refuse politely)
You were telling me about some murders?

INSPECTOR
Yes Miss Burrows, two you man were found dead on the M11. They were left there few miles away from each other. They were found yesterday late evening.

KATIE
I see. But why are you here. Do you think I had something to do with it?

SERGEANT
We are only making inquiries.

KATIE
But why come here. I had nothing to do with it.

INSPECTOR
Your car was seen on the M11 yesterday morning.

KATIE
Yesterday? It couldn't have been my car. I did not go out.

INSPECTOR
Are you sure about that?

KATIE
Of course I am. As a matter of fact I was putting it out in my diary.
(She takes the dairy and reads it)
Yesterday I had a good day. A very good day. I was alone all day while ....

(The Inspector interrupts her half way through)

INSPECTOR
That doesn't mean anything. That is only your say about and, excuse me for being blunt, but you could be lying.

KATIE
(Stands)
I do not lie. I hate that word and you should take it back.

INSPECTOR
I am sorry Miss, but it is my duty to ask these questions.

SERGEANT
Tell us again were you where yesterday.

KATIE
I was here all day, and that is the truth.

INSPECTOR
Can anyone vouch for that?

KATIE
No. I'm afraid not.

SERGEANT
You see our point Miss. You have no alibi. None at all.

KATIE
(Sits back)
Yes I know what you mean, but I am telling the truth.

INSPECTOR
We have to take your car away for a thorough inspection.

KATIE
What are you looking for. A weapon?
SERGEANT
No, I don't think so. I don't think we find any weapons, but traces of DNA maybe?

KATIE
(STANDS)
Are you sure you don't want a drink?

INSPECTOR
Thank you we are good.

KATIE
I have to get and get a glass of water.

INSPECTOR
By all means Miss go ahead.

KATIE
Thank you
(Exist)

SERGEANT
Are we sure she is the killer?

INSPECTOR
Not hundred per cent. But is it a coincidence that her car was also seen on that road when the other man was murdered three weeks ago? I did make much of it since they were no evidence pointing to it, but when her car was seen again yesterday travelling down the M11 I got very curious. The other cars checked were on seen once.

SERGEANT
Maybe she travels a lot down that way.

INSPECTOR
Many people do I know, but somehow I have a hunch.

SERGEANT
I hope you are right. The boss is expecting quick results.

INSPECTOR
He always does.

(We hear Katie and LOUISE shouting)
LOUISE
You stay here and I will deal with this. You a bloody coward.

KATIE
I'm afraid.

LOUISE
Why I am not surprised. Go to your room and stay there.

SERGEANT
(Surprised)
Who is she talking to?

INSPECTOR
I don't know. Maybe her……

(Enters LOUISE)

LOUISE
Good morning to you.

(They both stand)
INSPECTOR
And who are you?

LOUISE
(Laughs out loud)
The bitch…..She did not mention me?

SERGEANT
No, we thought she lived on her own.

LOUISE
That's what she wishes, but she is stuck with me. I am her twin sister.

INSPECTOR
Twin?

LOUISE
Yes, what so strange about that? We are not identical but we are twins.

INSPECTOR
I see.

LOUISE
Please be seated. I don't like to talk to people while standing.

(They sit)

SERGEANT
Do you have a car?

LOUISE
Of course I do.

INSPECTOR
What he means is do both of you have different cars.

LOUISE
No, I own the car, sometimes she borrows it.

INSPECTOR
I see. You car has been driving along the M11, yesterday? Was that you driving it?

LOUISE
Of course, Katie doesn't like driving the motor ways. She's a wimp you know.

SERGEANT
What were you going?

LOUISE
Shopping.

INSPECTOR
Shopping? Where?

LOUISE
London, where else?

SERGEANT
Where else!

INSPECTOR
Were there anything specific about your trip.

LOUISE
Excuse me. But why are you asking me all these questions?

SERGEANT
Your sister didn't mention it to you when she came to see you?

LOUISE
She did not come to see me. She came for a glass of water and I was there listening.

SERGEANT
Listening?

LOUISE
Yes listening.

INSPECTOR
In your journey did you have anyone with you in the car?

LOUISE
Let me see….

SERGEANT
There's nothing to see…. You should know…

LOUISE
Right you are and yes I had a man with me.

INSPECTOR
Your boyfriend, husband…

LOUISE
Who needs a husband! No, I don't know the man, I met him as I was having coffee in this establishment and he started to chat me up. I liked him so I didn't discourage him.

INSPECTOR
Can you describe him?

LOUISE
No mistaken. I never forget a man I like.

SERGEANT
And…

LOUISE
He was black! I think Jamaican of origin. I am not quite sure.

INSPECTOR
Do you always gift lifts to strangers.

LOUISE
Often. There's nothing wrong with that, is there?

INSPECTOR
No, no, no. It's your car and you can give lifts to anyone you want.

SERGEANT
Except it is not always safe. You don't know who they are.

LOUISE
Don't worry about me. I can take care of myself.

INSPECTOR
Where did you stop him.

LOUISE
Somewhere in London.
SERGEANT
And he was the only one you pick up.

LOUISE
What do you think I am a taxi driver?

INSPECTOR
I am surprised your sister did not mention it to you when she saw you in the kitchen.

LOUISE
We don't talk much. We hate each other. That is all.

INSPECTOR
So she did not mention the murders?

LOUISE
Murders?

SERGEANT
Two man.

LOUISE
I hope they were not good looking. It will be a waste.

INSPECTOR
As I said to your sister we have to take your car for some forensic test.

LOUISE
When?

INSPECTOR
Immediately.

LOUISE
What a shame.

SERGEANT
Why?

LOUISE
I was going to a party in Romford.

INSPECTOR
(Stands and so does the Sergeant)
I don't think you're going anywhere miss.

The door bell rings.

LOUISE
Excuse me, someone is a t the door.
(From outside)
You surely obey her don't you.
(She leaves and enters with the doctor)
(Introduces them)
This is Doctor Craig Flacks, our doctor.

(They exchange hands)

DOCTOR
Katie phoned me and told me to come because you were here.

SERGEANT
When did she do this?

LOUISE
When she came in for water, remember?

INSPECTOR
But why send for you?

DOCTOR
I knew the family very well, what you understand is….

INSPECTOR
Don't tell what I don't understand or not. This woman hear is suspect of murder.
(Louise Laughs)
I have to take her to the station now for more questions

DOCTOR
Have you got any proof about this.

LOUISE
Forget it doctor, don't try to save me now. Who cares about those men. All men are obsolete for me. They are a plague to us woman.

SERGEANT
Are confessing Miss.

LOUISE
(Sits seductively)
Are you a priest? If you are I will confess everything to you.

INSPECTOR
This is not a joke miss. It is extremely serious.

DOCTOR
But Inspector if you let me….

INSPECTOR
You can tell me after I interrogate her properly.

DOCTOR
If you just listen.....He moves to Louise and stands behind her)

INSPECTOR
Listen to what?

DOCTOR
To this.
(With his handkerchief he wipes off the red lipstick and pulls off the blonde wig from Louise's head, revealing Katie who becomes frightened and comforts herself tightly)
There are no sister inspector. Her name is Katie Louise Burrows. The most advance case of dual personality I have ever seen.

THE END

Printed in Great Britain
by Amazon

78171195R20031